North

STORIES AND PHOTOGRAPHS

Minnesota • Wisconsin • Michigan • Ontario

FOREWORD BY
Ron Schara

STORIES AND PHOTOGRAPHS BY

Dāv Kaufman, Dan Keyler, Bill Marchel , Barney Oldfield, Terry Pepper,
Kelly Povo, Jeff Richter, Phyllis Root, Martin Springborg

NORTH

Published by:
CROTALUS PUBLISHING
3500 Vicksburg Lane North #302
Plymouth, Minnesota 55447-1333
www.crotaluspublishing.com

Photography: ©1982-2004 Dāv Kaufman, Al Kaufman, Steven Gensler, Mitchell Gensler, Arnold Labofsky, Kelly Povo, Bill Marchell, Jeff Richter, Terry Pepper, Barney Oldfield, Martin Springborg.
Text: Forward ©2004 Ron Schara; "Those Four Days" ©2004 Dāv Kaufman; "North" ©2004 Phyllis Root; "In Search of Moose" ©2004 Martin Springborg; "Upper Mississippi Blufflands and Timber Rattlesnakes" ©2004 Dan Keyeler, "White Deer, Spirit Deer" ©2004 Jeff Richter, "Golden Hour" ©2004 Bill Marchel

ISBN 0-9741860-4-X

Art direction and project managment by Dāv Kaufman
Cover design and interior design by Marti Naughton
Book concept by Martin Springborg

COVER PHOTOS
FRONT: Bill Marchel (loon and bass fisherman), Barney Oldfield (rattlesnake),
Terry Pepper (lighthouse), Jeff Richter (deer)
FLAPS: Bill Marchel (wood duck and grouse)
BACK: Martin Springborg (moose), Kelly Povo (boundary waters)

Crotalus and the Rattlesnake Colophon are trademarks of Crotalus Publishing.
Library of Congress publishing data on record

First Printing, September 2004

Printed in China.

CONTENTS

Foreword
Ron Schara

Foreword

BY Ron Schara

As a journalist, Ron Schara has been sharing the great outdoor experience with his readers for nearly three decades. Over the years, as his newspaper and television popularity has grown, Ron's personality has become more a part of the fabric of the Midwest's outdoor community. A winner of four Emmy Awards, Ron is the commentator for many Minnesota radio and television stations, including his own program, *Minnesota Bound*, and his national program, *Backroads with Ron & Raven* on ESPN2, THE OUTDOOR CHANNEL, and local channels across the upper Midwest. He grew up loving the outdoors in northeast Iowa's rugged bluff country. He graduated with degrees in journalism and fish/wildlife biology and he has never veered from his ambition. Whether writing a newspaper story, talking with his radio and television audience, or appearing before a live audience, Ron Schara likes to use colorful storytelling to create a story for his audience. ww.mnbound.com or www.backroadswithron.com e-mail - ron@mnbound.com

Ron Schara photograph courtesy of Ron Schara Enterprises
Foreward photographs by Bill Marchel

AS A KID RAISED IN IOWA, it was fairly simple for me to define "north." To me, north was a vacation, a long journey by car. North was a vacation where you exchanged hard work, cow pastures and corn fields for clear, cool waters, majestic stands of pines, and a fighting fish on almost every cast. It felt cool to go north.

Those childhood memories stay with you. When I was 11 on one of those northern vacations, my Mother and I left our resort cabin, rowing out in the middle of a little nearby lake. The men, meanwhile, had left earlier that morning, traveling twenty-some miles to fish walleyes on Leech Lake. That afternoon they came back fishless, cold and soaked from the fierce wind. Mom and I greeted them with huge smiles, proudly holding up both ends of a stringer loaded with giant sunfish. I didn't get the last laugh, though; it was my first lesson in cleaning fish.

Now, older and wiser, my image of north isn't so simple. You can point north, you can head north and you can see north on a map. There's North Dakota, the North Star and - ho! ho! ho! - the North Pole.

But what is north, really? Can you explain north?

North can never be the same for any of us. For some, north is the quiet slip of a canoe paddle and the lonesome call of the loon, basking in nature as it was thousands of years ago. Others think of north as virgin territory waiting to be

explored, a lake waiting for the splash of its very first artificial lure, the chance to fool a monster fish. I've known some folks who wouldn't head north if you paved the way. Go figure.

In my line of work, I've met many people living "up north." They share our love of their territory, but have found a way to make a living. One of my favorite fishing guides, Woody (who is fairly reliable), has taken his passion and turned it into a business.

The north is a place where you escape, where you go to relax, to be closer to nature.

Yet the north isn't what it used to be. We haven't always been kind to things north. Does it seem to you we need to go farther north to get the same experiences?

The love and respect of all things north must be passed down to our children, and their children. Through conservation, catch-and-release, selective harvest and better ethics, our traditions and respect of things north can be brought back, preserved or saved for generations ahead.

North isn't just a place—but a mindset we must never lose.

Boundary Waters North

POEM BY Phyllis Root • PHOTOGRAPHS BY Kelly Povo

Phyllis Root [right], acclaimed children's writer with over 30 titles to her credit, has always loved the wilderness and its spiritual essence. She has canoed throughout the BWCA with family and friends for the past 20 years. Each of those trips has left an impression on her and has helped inspire her award-winning stories. She and friend Kelly Povo have taken several trips up north with their families, which sparked the idea for this book about their favorite place – the north woods.

Kelly Povo [left] has been a photographer for the past 25 years traveling across the country and throughout Europe and Mexico to find "Sacred Spaces" to photograph. She has found some of the most beautiful and sacred places right here in Northern Minnesota...the Boundary Waters Canoe Area...an area full of spirit and soul...an area pristine and pure and as beautiful as it was thousands of years ago. Traveling by canoe, with her Hasselblad camera, she has endeavored to capture the essence of place in these photographs—the stillness and serenity that can be found only in the wilderness.

To see more of Kelly's work check out www.kellypovo.com
And to read some of Phyllis's other works check out your local bookstore!

North is more than a point on the compass, a geographic location, a direction on the map.

North is a place in the imagination.

North is wild, unfettered, dangerous, enticing, silent, calm, rocky, snowy, inhabited by long-legged moose, lumbering bears, diving loons, soaring eagles, swimming beaver, sharp-toothed northern pike.

North is water and sky, sky and water, stitched together with bits of land and almost-hidden rocky paths from lake to river to lake. North is the Boundary Waters of northern Minnesota.

North is the northern lights undulating in the sky, flashing white, shifting to red, glowing green.

North is the full moon rising red as a forest fire.

North is the sky, when you get up to pee in the middle of the night, full of stars as big as chrysanthemums.

NORTH is the tart and tiny taste of blueberries found scattered on plants across a tiny, rocky islet.

North is the ancient picture writing on rock faces just at the height a person could reach to paint while standing in a canoe.

North is the even older art of rock and lichen and fern and moss painting the shore.

North is the twisted roots of old pines seemingly growing out of rock, the tiny seedlings of new pines finding bits of dirt to sprout in between the cracks in boulders or the decaying wood of down trees. How can anything grow in so little soil?

North is the bleached bones of a moose, the yellow markings in the snow of a pack of wolves, the flash of red as a fox disappears along the shore.

North is the silent diving of the loon and the wait for the loon to surface again, somewhere way out across the lake.

North is the tiny glimpse of pink corydalis, the nodding flower heads of pearly everlasting, the dark gleaming jewels of blue-bead lily.

North is the early morning light catching the beads of fog strung along a spider's web.

North is the cascading waterfall, the falling star, the driving rain; it is water endlessly seeking its way downhill,

answering the siren call of gravity, running finally to the sea.

North is the clip-clop of moose hooves on rock outside your tent at night, the buzz of hungry mosquitoes along the shore as you fish in the early morning.
North is the angry sneezy scolding of otters interrupted at their play, the yodeling calls of loons.

North is aching muscles and biting black flies and a headwind fighting you every inch of the way down the lake.
North is losing your way among the rocky inlets and coves and islands, of peering through the soaking, all-day rain as afternoon darkens
toward a pitch-black night. Is that really a campsite or just a bare spot on the rocks? Are you sure this is the way?

North is the terrible, long adrenaline rush of waiting for dawn and hoping it comes before the bear who has been terrorizing your tent returns.

North is sunrise at last.

North is a paddle, dipping into the water, pulling the canoe along one stroke, reaching forward, pulling, reaching, pulling, until the rhythm has always been a part of your body and you have been gliding over this lake, this water, forever.

North is finding your way by the lob-pine, the white pine towering, the dip in the tree line that might signal a portage.

North is stretching out on a sun-warmed rock, letting your muscles soak up heat and eternity.

North is following an overgrown trail to a place where you are sure no human has ever been before, only you, now, this minute.

North is the flickering fire that guides you home after an evening paddle into the darkening sky.

North is a quiet beauty, one that sneaks into your consciousness.

North is an emptiness that fills you up, a lifting of the heart, a certain knowledge of coming home even if you have never been here before.

North is a place in my soul.

In Search of Moose

STORY AND PHOTOGRAPHS BY **Martin Springborg**

Martin Springborg holds Bachelor and Master of Fine Arts degrees from the University of Minnesota, Twin Cities. A tireless artist and educator, he currently produces photographic works in his home studio in Saint Paul, and teaches photography and art history in college classrooms.

Place has infinite and often unknowable
influence on us. Speaking from an
artist's standpoint, I can say that my
work is made in direct response to the
many aspects of the place that I call
home. It is somewhat of an unending
dialogue, this conversation my work
has with Minnesota. And it has been
a long journey filled with many small
realizations that has brought me to this
understanding. Somewhere between a
search for a Northwoods icon and the
stillness of corn fields lay the nuances
of discovery.

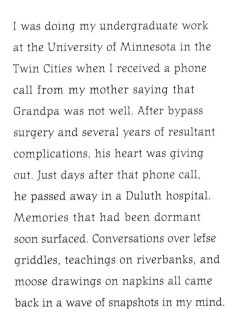

I was doing my undergraduate work
at the University of Minnesota in the
Twin Cities when I received a phone
call from my mother saying that
Grandpa was not well. After bypass
surgery and several years of resultant
complications, his heart was giving
out. Just days after that phone call,
he passed away in a Duluth hospital.
Memories that had been dormant
soon surfaced. Conversations over lefse
griddles, teachings on riverbanks, and
moose drawings on napkins all came
back in a wave of snapshots in my mind.

My grandpa was born and raised on the family farm in Middle River, a small Minnesota town filled with sunflowers, pine floors, work boots, and calloused hands. He carried on the tradition of farming that was handed down to him from his Norwegian parents until it became too difficult to make ends meet. He later moved his family to the Iron Range, where he worked as a carpenter on the construction of a taconite plant in Nashwauk. In 1965, work became scarce once again. He moved his family, including my mother, down to Monticello, Minnesota, so that he could take a job working on the construction of a nuclear power plant. My earliest memories of him take me back to my grandparents' house and to Monticello, the town where I was born and raised.

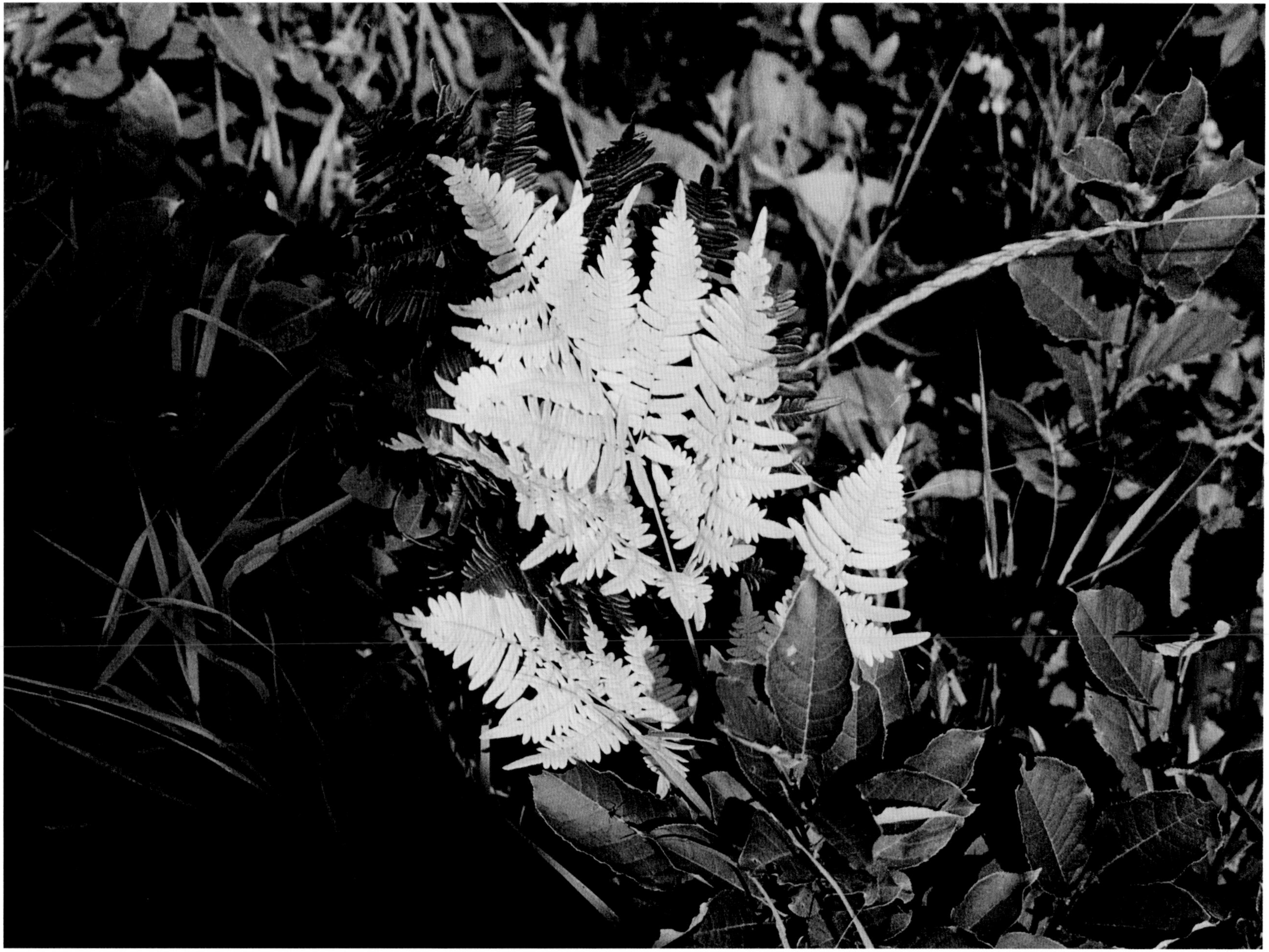

I remember Grandma's kitchen quite
vividly. Yellow and green, which I'm
sure was en vogue at the time. We used
to gather there for dinners, holidays,
birthdays, any and every occasion. In
fact, I can hardly remember eating in
my own house. It was in my grandma's
kitchen that my grandpa used to sit
with us grandkids at the yellow Formica
table and draw for us various animals on
paper napkins. Along with his drawings
came stories of the Northwoods. The
moose in those stories were always larger
than I could comprehend. The statement
"Why his head nearly cleared the garage
roof..." was not an unusual phrase. I also
heard about moose stepping over small
cars as they crossed the northern roads.
I was in awe of the animal's size in my
imagination, and I begged him to show
me one on our next trip to Middle River.
Alas, the moose eluded us. And when I
was much older and helped him and my
grandma move yet again—this time from
Monticello up to the Arrowhead region
of Minnesota, I watched the ditches and
the tree lines in anticipation of a large,
dark figure. Still nothing.

After Grandpa passed away, I made it
my quest to find the moose that he and
I were never able to see together. I
remember my first trip in search of the
illusive giant as though it were yesterday.
It was Halloween weekend of 1992. My
longtime friend, Dāv, and I set out for
Ely entranced by the idea of adventure
and survival in the wilds of Northern
Minnesota. With my uncle Doug at the
wheel, we bundled ourselves in every
bit of clothing we could scavenge from
our closets and braved the 250-mile ride
from Minneapolis in the covered-but-
quite-freezing bed of his pickup. We
played cards on the way up. I remember
breathing on them and watching as tiny
ice crystals formed around hearts, spades,
diamonds, and clubs.

By the time we reached my aunt and
uncle's house on Blueberry Lake,
our entry point into the wilderness,
it was late. The moon shone blue over
a crystallized landscape, and the air
was like a vacuum sucking in all sound.
All that could be heard was an intense
ringing in our ears; the sound of city
and freeway clashing with the calm
of Superior National Forest. We decided
in our infinite wilderness wisdom to
head straight out into the unknown in
the dark of night. We slid the canoe
out into the lake only to have it keep
on sliding on the thin sheet of ice that
had already begun to form. For more
than twenty yards, Dāv paddled in the
stern while I used my paddle to break
the ice over the bow. Open water sent
us on our way.

Once we reached an island, we built a
fire and sat listening in the quiet to the
many scrapes and scurries of small,
nocturnal animals and the occasional
"who cooks for you?" call from a far-off
barred owl. We slept under the stars, as
close as we could safely lie next to our
fire. I wore my sleeping bag around my
wool-cloaked body. In the morning I
found that my nose, the only part of
my body left exposed to the elements,
had acquired a thin layer of snow.

On our fist day of searching, we pain-
stakingly worked our way deep into
Superior National Forest. Not realizing
the importance of quiet, we made very
good time breaking through the underbrush on our way to a bog clearing.
Once the barrage of noise from our
tromping feet had ceased, we heard
the unmistakable sound of a moose
sloshing and cracking its way through
the woods somewhere off in the distance.
We stood frozen, listening intently,
until we heard nothing at all. I looked
down and snapped a photograph of
Dāv's feet surrounded by the evidence
that this animal had once stood in the
very spot we were now standing.

Many moose trips followed, and in as many places in Minnesota my search yielded nothing short of self-discovery. Truth be told, the most amazing things to come from looking for (and not finding so many) moose throughout these years lay in the many journeys taken in order to get myself in position to see them. I have discovered my home in my travels, most of the time spending a day or so traipsing around a shooting location and then taking off to go fishing, the smell of fish on my hands the marker of a good day. I've stood around many a bonfire with family in Ely, spinning stories of moose unseen. I've spent a frigid night on the Gunflint Trail in January after tracking a moose through snow up to my waist. I've canoed through countless lakes in the Boundary Waters, watched thousands of sunflower heads follow the sun in unison in Northwestern Minnesota, and dove from a raft made from plywood and plastic barrels into lake the color of rusted iron.

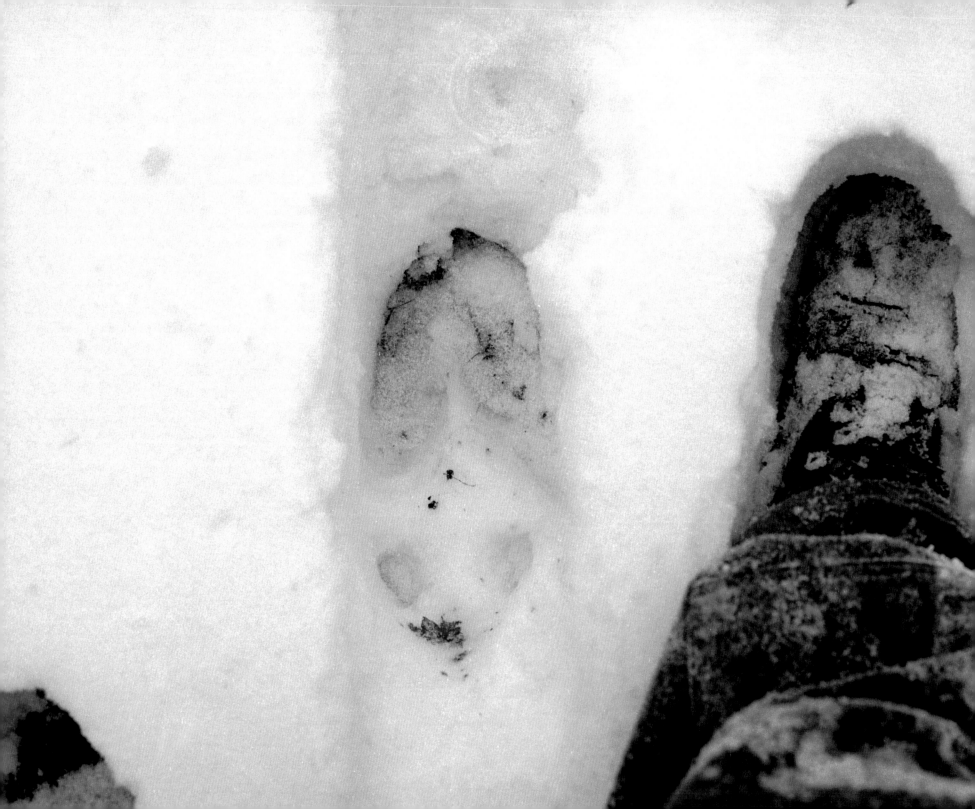

I've rowed past a pair of nesting loons whose greeting was so loud it deafened me into forgetting I had a camera around my neck, and spent the night in a yurt while listening to wolves howl outside my door. I've watched the wind sift through fields of corn while standing at my grandpa's grave. My grandpa. The man who set in motion my epic search for a great Minnesota icon. All of these experiences and so many more stem from the imaginings sewn in me by him. In my mind, he is woven into the iconography of this land.

N

44

And so it is fitting that my first moose were seen on a weekend trip to Middle River. Dāv and I were up at dawn one cold fall morning in Agassiz National Wildlife Refuge and making moose calls in the direction of a calm pond. We had both seen a glimpse of a moose the previous evening, but there was scarcely a photograph to be had through the windshield of the pickup. This time we waited, camera ready, in anticipation of some distant black silhouette. After calling for hours, I stopped and reached for my thermos of coffee. Looking up as I did so, I saw a young bull moose standing not 15 feet directly behind us. He looked bewildered, and perhaps a little lovesick. And for a bemused moment all three of us were frozen, he looking at us, we looking back at him from our perch on the bank of the pond. That is a picture that, although very much alive in my mind, was never meant to be on film. For in the time it took me to look back to my camera, he had already made his way across the road and deep into a thicket of willow.

Moose by Henry Wettestad, my grandpa

It was as though Grandpa were there
with me. I think he would have been
proud, and probably a little amused, to
see Dāv and I sitting there dumbstruck
at what had just transpired, both of us
watching the willow thicket for some sign
of that young bull's return. Now I have
my own stories to tell my grandchildren.
"Why, that bull must have stood at least
twice as high as our pickup..."

The Golden Hours

BY Bill Marchel

Bill Marchel of Fort Ripley, Minnesota is a full-time wildlife and outdoor photographer/ writer. His slide files contain over 90,000 images. Marchel has sold thousands of images—including over 100 magazine cover photos— to such prestigious magazines as Audubon, Field & Stream, National Wildlife, Outdoor Life and Ducks Unlimited. Bill's striking image of a great gray owl in flight, one of eleven of his photos that appeared in the Nov./Dec. 1997 issue of Audubon magazine, was a nature nominee for an Eisie Award, Life Magazine's The Best Magazine Photography of the Year. In 1998 and again in 2000, Marchel was awarded the People's Choice Award, Best of the Best Photography by the Outdoor Writers Association of America. His Web site is www.BillMARCHEL.com.

You are waist-deep in the water of a secluded lake. The sun is setting and the air is calm. A loon cries in the distance, broadcasting the end of the day. It's suppertime for largemouth bass so your senses are keen as you cast a surface lure to an open pocket in the bulrushes.

Fire and ice. Even thought the sky is ablaze with warm colors and the ice is glowing like oak embers in a hot fire, your toes tingle and your fingers are numb. But on a hill along a distant shoreline, the lights have just come on at the ski resort, and you're sure the skiers enjoying the slopes are warmer than you. Maybe tomorrow.

Bowhunters know their quarry is most active at dusk. It's the whitetail witching hour, so we maximize our efforts by hunting at that time. And if no game appears, a brilliant setting sun often rewards our labors.

Those Four Days

BY Dāv Kaufman

Dāv Kaufman is an accomplished filmmaker and novelist. Referring to his first novel, *Lake Desire*, based from his screenplay of the same name, he has been called "a novelist of considerable and original talent."–Midwest Book Review. As a filmmaker, he has produced several independent films of all genres. He has also written and directed several short films and music videos. His writings range from freelance magazine articles to scripts for both television and film. After living and working in the film industry in Los Angeles, Dāv moved back to his native Minnesota longing for the unique outdoor culture and pine-laden lakeshores only found in the North. He continues to write and make movies today, but now happily from a lakeshore instead of the seashore.

I was thirteen when I first saw the Shield lakes of Ontario, Canada. With my face pressed against the dirty window in the back of an old Winnebago, I was silent in my own wonderment as I stared out into a boreal splendor I had only before imagined. I had waited all my life to go on that trip, just like all the other boys in the family. Since 1953, when my father was thirteen, it had been a family tradition that at the hallowed age of thirteen our right of passage into manhood would be via a fishing boat somewhere on Lake of the Woods. For me, those thirteen years of anticipation culminated in 1982.

Growing up in Minneapolis, meaning "lake city" in a Greek and Dakota word combo, I thought that I had seen every kind of lake there was. But with the first glances over the azure water and emerald pines of Lake of the Woods, I was surprised at feeling cheated for having been deprived that majesty all my life. Closing my eyes to allow the first images of that lake to burn into my memory, I realized I had never known what a lake really was before I saw that one. And now, twenty-two years later, the image of that first encounter remains as vivid as it did then.

Of the many things that I have grown to love about the region known as the Canadian Shield, the phenomenon of time having no forward motion is the one I hold most treasured. Those four days we spend there each year are not owned by time or calendar or work or obligation. Those four days are our days, and in them, we are all thirteen again.

That morning in 1982, as I left Minneapolis with my uncle Elliott, my father Al, and my three cousins—Steve, Mickey, and Arnie—I waved goodbye to my mother who stood in the driveway waving back with my sister and my brother, who, although he's two-and-a-half years older than I, fishing just wasn't his thing, and he didn't join us for the first time until 1986. I looked at each of them as the camper pulled away, saying my own goodbyes, knowing that the next time I saw them, it would no longer be as a boy. My dad's sister was nine years older than he was, creating a gap in age between me, my siblings, and my cousins. That left me the youngest in the group by twelve years, and to this day, I can trace back the origins of the more colorful aspects of my vocabulary to that trip.

UNCLE ELLIOTT, ARNIE,
MICKEY, STEVE, ME & DAD
1982

DAD & ME
1984

THE GANG
1985

After crossing the border into Canada, I never left my seat near that dirty window, and likewise, the awe implanted on my face never left either. Noticing this, my father came and sat next to me. "It's quite something, isn't it?" he said, putting his arm on my shoulders, his voice reflecting the same awe with which I was overcome. I could only nod in return. He smiled at me as if through my eyes, he, too, was seeing it for the first time. "Tomorrow morning, you'll be right out there fighting a fish bigger than you are. Think you're ready?"

Was I ready? For thirteen years I had been ready. Months before that, the day after my thirteenth birthday, with winter still in full effect, I had planted a coffee can in the snow in the backyard, and practiced casting with a daredevil from which I had removed the hooks. I was out there everyday after school, timing it perfectly for my father's arrival home from work, so he could see me out there practicing for the trip.

By the renaissance of spring, I was able to throw a lethal cast, but I waited to show it off until the day my father finally joined me. As he clipped the casting weight to the end of his line, he looked down at me

with a look that playfully challenged me to prove to him that I was ready for the trip.

My upper lip stiffened as I prepared myself. I knew he would be impressed if I managed to get even close to the can; anywhere within six inches would be good enough, I figured. Holding my breath, I pinched the line against the rod with my index finger, and slowly flipped the bail, while offering a silent imploration to the wind to remain at my back. I inhaled, held it, and squinted a bead on the can twenty yards in front of us. Then I cast, and sailed the spoon directly into the can. The hollow clank reverberated across the yard echoed by my father's roar of amazement. "Wha-hoo! You put that puppy right in the can! Outstanding!" For some reason, my father called everything "puppy". I guess it was just his thing, but it always made me chuckle when he said it.

Truth be known, I was more surprised than he was—in my months of practice, I had never before hit a bulls-eye; but I never did tell him that. From that day until we left for the trip, we made a ritual of afternoon meetings in the backyard with a coffee can and an old daredevil. It was

Good Day Fishin'
1986

Stephen & Me
1986

1988

our sacred time together as father and son, and the closest we got to Canada without actually being there. I never did get another bulls-eye, but as far as both of us were concerned, I didn't need to.

Two weeks before we were to leave, Dad and I would take a ritual inventory of the tackle box on the kitchen table. We frolicked through that box like two kids who had just found an old shoebox full of baseball cards as we separated all the hooks, jigs, and everything else into designated piles. Each lure had its own stats, and my imagination grew ferocious as he held up a big red and white daredevil that proudly displayed the scars of battle across its painted face.

"This one caught a northern so big I could hardly get that puppy into the boat! She was as big as my leg, and I'll be damned if she didn't spit the hook at the last minute. Then, five minutes later, your cousin Mickey caught the same damn fish on another red and white daredevil! You should have seen the look on my face when he landed it. I was pissed and pleased at the same time!" I cherished cleaning out that tackle box, and hearing those stories almost as much as going on the trip itself.

At that age, it was one of those rare times that I actually listened to what my father had to say, and through those conversations, we bonded in a way we never had before.

Of course, even with an overstuffed box of indefectible lures, we still managed to justify a trip down to the local bait shop to load up on everything we both knew we didn't need for the trip, but got anyway just for the fun of it. Mostly we just went there to gawk and dream at the trophies on the walls; at least I did. There's a truth that bait shops are where dreams are born from the imaginations of those with ample wall space, and my father ignited my imagination as he saw that I was staring up at a particularly big northern. "You catch one, I'll mount it for you," he said with a tone that seemed to guarantee that I'd have a fish bigger than that one on my wall in a few weeks. My eyes could only grow wider, and as they did, his smile grew larger. Every night from that day on, I was lulled to sleep with images of huge muskies, northerns, and walleyes as under my covers with a flashlight, I read every article in every fishing magazine I could find.

DAD, ME & ARNIE
1989

DAD & ME
1992

JOSH
1993

We arrived at the lodge well after dark that first night. Lying in bed in that cabin amidst the mingling odors of mildew and some pine-scented cleanser, I was too energized to sleep. I was there. The wait was over. Tomorrow was sure to be the greatest day of my thirteen-year-old life. But at that moment, there was nothing I could do but impatiently stare out the window at the indigo sky, hoping the sun magically would rise sooner than any other morning. That night seemed to last forever.

When morning finally did arrive, we headed to the rustic mess hall for a breakfast of army food and hot coffee before meeting our guides and loading the boats for the forty-minute ride to that magical walleye hole in the middle of the lake. At our first stop, I began to rummage through the tried and tested lures in our box, making a direct grab for that beaten and scarred red and white daredevil. Noticing this, the guide simply looked straight at me, shook his head, and said "jig and a minnow." Then he grabbed the end of my line and affixed a lead-head jig and a rather lively rainbow minnow. "All you do is jig it off the bottom, ay?

Make it seem that the minnow's more lively than the other minnows down 'ere that don't have a hook through their lips," he said with a personal little laugh. "When ya feel that there's a little extra weight, set the hook, ay? That's all 'ere is to it," he continued, then threw my line over the side of the boat.

A bit confused, and even more distraught, I nevertheless did as he instructed. "Wait a minute," I thought, "I've been practicing casting for months, and now we're just going to jig like catching sunnies off the dock? What the hell was this bullshi-" and then my rod doubled over. I set the hook, and after a pretty decent fight, I pulled up my first walleye. My father threw his hands up in the air with a cheer that could be heard across the lake. "That's my son! The first fish of the trip, caught by my son! Hold it up!" he said as he pointed his waiting camera at me. A quick flash, and then he turned to everyone else in the boat. "You see that?! That's my son, right there. My son!" From that point on, I really didn't mind this new technique, especially after we all limited out after a few short hours.

DAD & STEPHEN
(& OUR GUIDE)
1995

MARC, BRENT
DAD & STEVE
1995

DAD & BRENT
1996

The afternoon found us casting in shallow weedy bays for northerns, where out of all the new and old lures in our box, I never threw anything else but that old beat-up red and white daredevil. Each small northern I pulled in reaffirmed that this place was as sacred as I had imagined it would be. At some point, I looked at my father, who looked back at me with a smile; I knew that he felt it as well. And that's what we had. There was little else in our lives that we had in common—even at age thirteen, I knew that about us. But we had Canada. We had those four days in common to truly be father and son.

With that realization, I put down my rod and just sat, absorbing the serenity of that time and place. It electrified my senses as the call of a white-throated sparrow echoed from the pines, followed by the lonesome call of a loon. Still now, and surely forever, those two calls will be synonymous with a shallow weedy bay somewhere in the middle of both nowhere and heaven.

I returned from that first trip to my mother, sister and brother standing in the driveway much like we had left them. Slowly stepping from the camper, I wondered if they might notice a difference in me. Seeing my mother and sister recoil at the lingering smell of stale cigar smoke and pungent old fish that saturated my clothes, I knew right at that moment, that I had, in fact, become a man. I hadn't come home with a trophy for the wall, but what I did come back with was a stronger connection to my dad than any we had previously shared. That, in and of itself, was a greater trophy than anything I could have pulled out of that lake.

Since that first excursion, my father and I missed only two trips until 1998. One was the next year in 1983 because of my mother's cousin's wedding (we lost a bet), and the other in 1987 when my Uncle Elliot passed away. The one time we broke from tradition was in 1993, when we said goodbye to the lodge that the family had gone to for forty years, and we upgraded our accommodations to Totem Resorts in Sioux Narrows. Since then, my brother Stephen, who I believe would love the outdoors more if it came equipped with a high-speed modem, has been with us a half dozen times. As it was with my father, the trophy I return with those years is what's been won fishing alongside him, as for those four days, we become closer friends than most other brothers ever get to be.

STEPHEN & ME
1997

BRENT & ME
1998

ME, JOSH
BRENT & MARC
2000

Our tradition carries on into yet another generation. Arnie's son, Josh joined us for the first time in 1993, and the following year, my cousin Steve's son Marc, joined us. Two years later, Marc's younger brother, Brent, joined us. With their arrivals, my father had found three new reasons to love fishing in Canada. While teaching his nephews to fish, he had a wonderful habit of quietly setting the hook, then announcing that there was something wrong with their reels, and that he'd fix it if they would hold his. After the handoff, my cousin's faces would light up as they realized they had fish on the line. I don't think Dad pulled up a fish for himself for years.

On that lake, surrounded by family, my father enjoyed that place like nowhere else. Those four days had become so sacred to us, that even as he lay on that hospital bed back in 1998, I told him as I tried to smile some sort of reassurance into him, that we would be sitting in a fishing boat in Canada in a few months, laughing about how scared he was making all of us. The doctors then took him back into surgery to try and catch the clots that were ransacking his arteries. But they missed one.

Four hours later, minutes after he returned from the operating room, I stood in the doorway of his room with my brother, sister, and mother helplessly watching his heart monitor flatline as the doctors and nurses tried to resuscitate him. It wasn't until a long time after that, when the haze of despair had lifted, that I recalled those last words I said to him—"We'll be fishing in Canada soon, Dad." He was gone to fast for me to say anything else to him. But I don't know that I needed to. Those four days were so important to us that I like to think that no other words could have said how much he meant to me. I like to think it was how I told him I loved him.

Tradition is the strength that holds families together, and for those four days, our tradition is fishing as it has been in our family for fifty years. The tradition continues as Mickey's son Elliot joined us for the first time in 2002, followed by Arnie's new son-in-law, David. My nephew Jared is next in line to go. Now only eight, he talks about it all the time just as I had at his age. And, being his uncle, soon I'll be joining him and his father in the backyard with a particular scarred-up daredevil and a coffee can.

ME & JOSH
2001

FAMILY
2002

ELLIOT
2003

If time has not touched that lake since Glacial Lake Agassiz drained and left behind a puddle we named Lake of the Woods, then for those four days, nothing will change for us as well. Everyone is still young. Everyone is still with us. And therefore, every year, for those four days, I get to fish with my father once again.

DAD AND HIS
RED AND WHITE
DAREDEVIL

Upper Mississippi Blufflands and Timber Rattlesnakes

STORY BY **Dan Keyler** • PHOTOGRAPHS BY **Barney Oldfield**

For the past 8 years, Barney Oldfield has been a practicing veterinarian in New Mexico. Previous to this he lived in Minnesota for nearly 20 years pursuing dairy practice in Goodhue, Minnesota. During his stay in Minnesota, he became engaged in a number of conservation programs with native reptiles and amphibians including Timber Rattlesnakes and Wood Turtles. He served as chairman for an anti-bounty committee that successfully ended the Minnesota rattlesnake bounty program. He was photographer and coauthor for the book "Amphibians and Reptiles Native to Minnesota" published by the University of Minnesota Press in 1994. He continues to pursue conservation and field studies of reptiles with an emphasis on rattlesnakes and collared lizards.

Photo of Barney Oldfield with a non-venomous Fox snake ©Casey Oldfield

Dan Keyler grew up along the banks of the Tippecanoe River in Indiana where encounters with snakes were common. During his high school years Dan's scientific interest in venomous snakes was greatly influenced by the late Dr. Sherman Minton. After graduation from Purdue University he moved to Minnesota for advanced professional education at the University of Minnesota. Based in Minneapolis, Dr. Keyler is a toxicologist with Hennepin County Medical Center and the Minneapolis Medical Research Foundation. He consults on the medical treatment of venomous snakebites nationally, and does research in the discipline of immunotoxicology. He has been studying timber rattlesnake distribution, reproduction, and genetics in the Upper Mississippi River Valley for 20 years.

From the high point of solid rock on which I stood, the vast Upper Mississippi River Valley stretched as far as the eye could see. Reflecting the rising sun, the river trailed like a wide silver ribbon embellishing the landscape along its peaceful flow to a hazy southern horizon. The series of Minnesota-Wisconsin bluffs, their long east-west running ridges separated by deep valleys, reached like dark green fingers tipped with tan nails to the banks of the Mississippi, the father of rivers. The sun's rays warmed my face, and the late summer humidity already was causing sweat beads to form above my eyes. It was August, and I was about to begin another day of late-season fieldwork. My true professional life as a clinical and research toxicologist at a large medical center and biomedical research foundation for the past twenty years has been rewarding, but it has been this fieldwork that has always claimed my passion. Standing on that lookout at dawn, I was struck as always by the spectacular vista. Most folks traveling to northern Midwest states are destined for the Boundary Waters, the North Shore, the Apostle Islands, Bayfield, or other northland wilderness areas. Yet, I always have preferred the Mississippi blufflands and the associated small river corridors of southeastern Minnesota and western Wisconsin. It's there I've enjoyed studying the unusual and least-liked creatures that haunt the rugged terrain where few people venture.

In our lower 48 states it's hard to find an American who hasn't heard legendary stories of the timber wolf, that controversial and well-known predator that frequents the northern woodlands of Minnesota and Wisconsin. However, few Americans, including most Minnesotans and Wisconsinites, are aware of an equally notorious counterpart found in the bluffs and caverns along the upper Mississippi in the more southerly parts of these states. To those who do know of it, the timber rattlesnake is just as legendary as its northern namesake. Usually rattlesnakes are thought of as varmints associated with big ranches in Texas and Arizona, not with the rich green valleys and bluffs hundreds of miles to the north of the hot southern deserts and arid mountains. With these thoughts rambling through my mind, I realized it was time to stop pondering and begin the day's work of intense surveying for the elusive timber rattlesnake. First, however, I pulled out my cell phone (something I wouldn't have been able to do in earlier years of field surveying) and made a call to New Mexico. I couldn't resist letting my longtime field research partner, Dr. Barney Oldfield, know what a beautiful morning it was on the Mississippi bluffs, and that I was sure I would have exciting things to report at the end of the day.

Barney, as entranced by the timber rattlesnake as I am, had been my field partner and ever-constant snake photographer for nearly fifteen years of never-ending research of this unique animal. He had moved to the Southwest (down where rattlesnakes are far more abundant and more frequently encountered), leaving his large animal veterinary practice in Hiawatha Valley, to return to his roots and fulfill his dream of being proprietor of his own animal hospital, the Totah Pet Clinic. I was lucky with my chance call; Barney actually answered the phone. Upon hearing where I was, he responded with envy, and I detected a little melancholia as well. After a few words, and repeated interruption in the communication signal, Barney said, "Keep your eyes open, make sure you take some fluids along, be careful, and watch your step."

Searching for timber rattlesnakes in their own element is no easy task. Along with the beautiful scenery, there are a few constant nuisances. You get sweaty, dirty, covered with ticks, swarmed by mosquitoes, and stung by hornets, all to end up with very sore ankles and legs from hiking across 50-degree slopes all day in the heat! You're also apt to end up crawling on hands and knees along ledges barely wide enough to support you. At times they don't, or you slip, and you find yourself desperately grabbing at sumac stems, grass, or whatever you can find to hang on to. It's then you look down, realize it is a long way to the base of the bluff, look back up and put mind, muscle, and strain into getting back to where you were. Also it's important to be aware of where you are placing your hands, lest you disrupt a napping rattlesnake. Fortunately, timber rattlesnakes usually don't strike unless your hand is a direct plant on the snake, but you do have to back up cautiously. At times camera gear and field gear go for a flying, tumbling ride, leaving you to pray that nothing ends up broken. Overall, however, you gradually become quite tolerant of these inconveniences, and learn to continue your search without a second thought.

When fatigue or heat demand the need for rest, it's an opportunity to sit down, relax, and take note of surroundings and scenery that in my mind just don't get any better. The uniqueness of the bluff ecosystem is evident in the flora that thrives there: compass plants, pasque flowers, fringed orchids, big bluestem and Indian grasses. The rock structure, primarily composed of dolomite and Jordan sandstone, provides a meager substrate for the bluff prairie plants, and importantly, is intermittently dispersed with rock fissures and horizontal crevices, creating seasonal resorts for the timber rattlesnake. Expanses of oak, maple, and hickory forests shelter the locusts and katydids that create the surrounding valley's hum. It's simple to understand—to feel—why Native Americans loved these river blufflands. Sometimes, you find yourself resting, and as you sift the dry soil, point flakings of white and gray flint run through your fingers reminding you this was once the camp of others, confirming an unknown presence, and making it easy to let your mind drift back in time. At such times I find myself wondering, how many timber rattlesnakes were living here 200-300-500 years ago when early explorers navigated the Mississippi?

When we began looking for timber rattlesnakes in the region twenty years ago, it was only for the pure interest of finding and observing a rattlesnake in the wild in one of the most unlikely geographic regions of our country for rattlesnakes to inhabit. It took about three years, and many painfully failed attempts before we began to learn where these snakes lived, and depending on the season, when they were likely to be seen. Then, in 1988, we applied for a research grant to study the distribution of timber rattlesnakes in upper western Wisconsin, and were lucky enough to have it awarded. That was the beginning of our realization that we knew little about timber rattlesnakes in the blufflands of the Upper Mississippi River Valley of Minnesota and Wisconsin. From talking with a few old-time bounty hunters we learned where the snakes made their homes, or had in years past. Interestingly, as our research continued, we discovered that the snakes had been hunted to extinction in some areas, not out of pure maliciousness, but as a way of life in the river blufflands. Hunting the timber rattlesnake was a tradition that had been passed from generation to generation. Historically, our States paid bounties to have rattlesnakes killed, and the bounties collected even helped to sustain some families during the depression years earlier in the 20th century. Thus, the complex interface of man, rattlesnakes, and the blufflands has contributed an interesting chapter in the history of the Upper Mississippi River Valley.

As I stood on the bluff that day, however, my purpose was clear: I would survey one of the historical rattlesnake sites and look for old friends, timber rattlesnakes I had studied over the seasons in years past. Locating timber rattlesnakes in late summer is a bit more challenging than in early May when they emerge from seven months of hibernation, and tend to stay around their den site for awhile before their initial forage for food. Now, however, it was late August, and I would search in particular for maternal females that hopefully had given birth to young rattlesnakes. Timber rattlesnakes are not like birds or mice, or even deer, animals that mature rapidly and begin reproducing from the age of a few months to a couple of years. Northern timber rattlesnakes may take five to eight years to reach a reproductive age, and they may reproduce only every three to four years, giving live birth to litters of five to ten young. Timber rattlesnakes will mate in late summer the year before they give birth, which takes place in late August and early September of the following year. This uniquely slow reproductive cycle makes the timber rattlesnake a species highly vulnerable to disrupting factors that have little impact on the survival of other animal species.

It was now 0930 hours and the sun was high enough to begin warming the eastern and southeastern facing slopes of the bluff prairies. Looking across to other bluffs I noticed how the sun defined the stony out-crops among the green hills. My plan was to start at the top of the bluff and gradually work my way downward in a wide travers-ing pattern. I'd just begun when out of the corner of my left eye, I saw a movement in the knee-high grass and heard a slight rustle. You don't always spot timber rattlesnakes with your eyes; often you hear them first, slowly slithering through the grass or leaves. This alarm however, was nothing more than a blue racer gliding along effort-lessly, and as I turned to take a closer look, it darted down the slope and rapidly disap-peared into the landscape.

Soon I approached a small cluster of rocks warmed by the sun, but I saw no signs of a rattlesnake—no crawl tracks, no shed skins, no depressions in the grass next to rocks where snakes may have been lying. When you come upon these rock formations you always have to approach slowly, cautiously, remembering that snakes sense your movement through the vibration of the ground, even when they can't see you approaching. Looking up, I checked the cedar trees, where on several past occasions I had found timber rattlesnakes resting in the branches, observing me as I surveyed the ground below. As I crept on my knees, face sideways to the ground, peering under a small rock lip, I noticed first the white chin, then the head of an adult timber rattlesnake. Time, 1047 hours.

Motionless, we stared at each other, eye-to-eye. Then the snake's tongue began to flicker, sensing the air chemistry, trying to figure out how much of a threat I might be. As my eyes adjusted to the light, I saw next the head of a newborn rattlesnake at the left of the small crevice. Soon I saw more little heads; I counted five total. The mother, still focused on me, did not move or attempt to strike. Squinting, and looking closer, I noticed the vertical black stripe running up and down the central groove of the tan rattle. Ah ha! This was a snake that had been marked on its rattle two years previous, and was now making a critical contribution to the survival of this bluffland species in the river valley. Awestruck, I thought, few people would compare this scene to one of a cat with a litter of kittens, but these young timbers, fully equipped to survive, would stay as a litter with their "Mom" for about two weeks before heading out on their own. They would shed their skins for the first time during this period, changing from dull gray to light brown, the bulk of their bodies decorated with a series of black chevron bands running down towards their tails, where it becomes a velvety black, and they gain their first rattle segment. I would not disturb the peaceful group, but vividly imprint the image in my mind's eye. It was now 1200 hours, time to move away from the rookery, find a somewhat comfortable grassy place to lie back, and take a brief nap.

As I lay staring up with one eye at the bright sky, a red-tailed hawk soared the thermals. Soon I drifted off to sleep and into wonderful rest—that is, until awakened by what felt like hundreds of little needle-sharp teeth biting at my legs. Jumping up, I frantically brushed and slapped against my field fatigues. My luck, I had napped over an anthill in the grass and the little rascals had made their way up inside my baggy fatigues. Nature's way, I guess, of letting me know that too much napping is not a good way to accomplish your fieldwork.

The "ants in my pants" situation remedied, I still had about half of the bluff to survey, and the heat was becoming rather intense. I slugged down some water and began wading across the bluff through the sumac, ninebark, and Indian grass. I have often wondered how many snakes I pass by without seeing them, yet knowing they are watching me. Rock outcrop to rock outcrop I searched, but no timber rattlesnakes. At intervals, my gaze turned toward the cool, lazy Mississippi far below, noting the sandy towheads at the tips of the small river islands. I could feel the waters coolness, and thought how nice a quick dip in the river would feel. I came to my senses, put my daydreaming aside, and made my way to the sandstone at the base of the bluff. The shadows of the surrounding trees were now intermittently cast over rocks, still warm from several hours of constant sun, and the calm air held only the soft chirping of field crickets.

A small slab of sandstone jutted out from the slope, draped with wild grape vine. After years of working with timber rattlesnakes you develop a sixth sense with which you can feel their presence even before seeing them. Still, if my eyes had not been well-trained from years of observing the cryptic nature of timber rattlesnakes, I wouldn't have noticed the large rattlesnake with its black chevrons, bordered by sulfur yellow, lying motionless beneath the grapevine, dappled with scattered light, and partially concealed by a crevice. It did not move; I did not move. The elliptical pupils of its eyes watched me; the large tan rattle rested next to its head. I noticed the rattle had no vertical black marking, meaning this snake had eluded us in previous field seasons. This field encounter would change that fact. I gently placed my snake hook under its belly and swiftly hoisted it out into the open grass on the slope. This, the snake did not like, and it immediately began to rattle a rapid buzz reminiscent of the sound of steam being released from my mom's old pressure cooker.

I thought of Oldfield, far off in New Mexico, and wished he were here to help contain the snake for marking and gathering biological data. But he wasn't, so the task was mine alone. Getting out my largest snake tube, Barney's words from our morning chat ran through my mind: "Be careful." I'd need to maneuver the open end of the tube, basically a piece of thin, clear Plexiglas pipe about 1½ inches in diameter by two feet long, over the head of the snake. If all goes well, the snake will actually crawl into the tube thinking it is crawling into a hiding hole. You do however, have to make sure you don't use too large a diameter tube on too small a snake, because the snake will make a u-turn and bite your hand. As soon as the snake was in the tube, I grabbed its body and the lip of the tube together. This allowed me to examine the snake without injuring it, and without it injuring me. I documented biologic data: length 45 inches from the tip of its snout to the base of the rattle; body temperature 29C;

probed to be a male (snakes have a cloaca that conceals the sex organs, but that can be probed to determine its depth—males probe to greater depth); rattle, 11 segments; positive post ocular bar (dark diagonal bar marking behind the eye); and a prominent mid-dorsal stripe (usually a rust colored stripe which runs the length of the snake's back bone). I marked the rattle with a permanent marker, and then emptied the snake from the tube into a nylon bag in order to weigh it. The big guy weighed 1.4 kg. All together, a fairly sizeable adult male timber for the river valley area!

If my New Mexican side-kick had been with me on this excursion, the data collection would have been followed by an Oldfield photo session in which Barney, camera in hand and stretched out on his stomach, would be asking, "How close am I to the snake?" at the same time I was suggesting he back up a little. But Barney loved close-up shots, and never resisted the opportunity to attain yet another. Having no camera and not being a photographer of the Oldfield caliber, I moved right on to what for me is the best part of the whole process—releasing the snake to freedom at exactly the site from which I'd extracted it. Slowly, I lifted the base of the nylon bag, cautiously avoiding where the snake's head was, and gently slid the snake back onto the grapevine-covered rock. Without a single rattle, it crawled quietly back into the crevice, probably wondering if it had all been just a bad dream.

It had been a fulfilling encounter, but the late afternoon light was quickly fading, as was my energy, and I still had a long hike back out to the vehicle followed by the several hour drive back to the less enjoyable realities of civilization. I needed to be on my way, but first, I took one last, long look: shortening shadows evidenced the fading sun even as its warm amber light softly lighted the bluffs across the river. "Maybe next year," I thought "Oldfield will be back here." Then I turned to leave, filled with the same sense of rejuvenation I always felt after sharing a day with the land, the river, and the timber rattlesnake—a day in Minnesota's blufflands of the Upper Mississippi River Valley.

White Deer, Spirit Deer

STORY AND PHOTOGRAPHS BY Jeff Richter

Jeff Richter's fascination with the woods and wildlife led to early careers as a logger and a trapper. Then in the spring on 1990, he put the traps away and picked up a camera. "I saw photography as a natural transformation to maintain my love of observing and exploring wild places." Jeff has won numerous awards, both regional and national, including as I.R.M.A. Award from the International Regional Magazine Association for his photos of albino deer in 2001. Two of the images were finalists in the British Gas/BBC International Wildlife Photographer of the year award in 2002. Jeff's photos have appeared in books, magazines, calendars, and posters in the Nature Conservancy, Audubon, Sierra Club, Wisconsin Trails, and a host of others. He currently lives with his wife Rosy in Boulder Junction, Wisconsin where they run their gallery "Nature's Gallery."

Most nature photographers have an un-ending curiosity about the plant and animal communities, and the ecosystems that they spend countless hours observing and photographing. Occasionally, a specific subject seems to capture one's imagination. Whether it's a particular species of animal or perhaps a region of the country, for some reason it grabs you by the scruff of the neck, shakes you, and leaves you a little dazed. Such was the case some years ago when I became aware of a population of albino deer in northern Wisconsin.

Historically, there was mention of white deer or elk in journals all the way back to the days of Marquette and Joliet. Then, back in the 1940's a photographer from Life magazine took a picture of an albino deer near Boulder Junction, Wisconsin that was used for the cover. Since those early days there have existed pockets of albino deer throughout the North, due at least in part, to their protected status in Wisconsin. Most states have not extended them protection; perhaps worrying they would weaken the herd. Thankfully for all of us, Wisconsin was able to see the big picture and recognize the unique-ness of these creatures.

For me the fateful day came when I walked into a small fern-covered opening in a near-by woods and came face to face (except for a camera, lens and film in-between) with my first albino deer and was instantly hooked. There is something visually striking, even a little startling about seeing this pure white creature against the rich greens of our summer forest. Despite their attempts at conceal-ment they are so alarmingly obvious it's almost comical. For several years I spent a considerable portion of my time, energy and film pursuing various albino deer at numerous albino deer at numerous locations throughout the seasons.

Encounters ranged from almost
being able to feed them by hand,
to instantly disappearing at first
glance. From the stark full-light
of mid-day to the twilight of a
descending fogy evening, where
they appeared as a spirit moving
ghost-like through a medieval,
old-growth forest, literally ending
chills up my back. No two sightings
were ever the same.

As with photographing any wild
animals, the behavior of individuals
varies greatly from day to day. That
was illustrated by a buck, which I
spent a lot of time with. His territory
became familiar enough that I could
locate him about 50% of the time.
When I did find him his behavior
would range from hardly reacting
to my presence to getting nothing
but glimpses of his rear-end
disappearing into the densest
underbrush or swamp he could
find, until I got discouraged. No
matter what I learned about his
habits he always kept me guessing.

Truthfully, that ever-changing aspect
of animal behavior is one of the great
attractions in my photographic pursuit
of any wildlife. Trying to understand
and anticipate actions before they
occur is a big part of successful shooting. Moreover, the attempt to factor
in all the external stimuli; like weather
conditions, seasonal changes, other
animals, both friend and foe, previous
human encounters, all affect the way
your subject is going to react at any
given moment. Having a sense, a feel,
a guess really, as to what your subject
is about to do allows the photographer
precious seconds to compute some of
the technical aspects (exposure, aperture,
and backgrounds) in producing a strong
image. For me it's endlessly challenging,
frustrating and ultimately rewarding,
when everything clicks.

I'm not enough of a geneticist to understand what causes these unique deer. I'm not even sure if there are true albinos or not. Despite their pink noses and cream-colored hooves (instead of the normal black) I've never seen one that had pink eyes, which many people say is the only way it can be a true albino. Really, it doesn't matter except from a purely scientific viewpoint. More interesting to me is that I've seen normal brown does with white fawns and I've seen white does with both brown and white fawns. The newborn fawns I've seen actually had a slight cream coloration along with the normal spotting of brown fawns. Gradually the cream fades after a few months, until they become pure white. Their behavior when around other deer ranged from being completely ostracized to exhibiting dominance over the group. Rarely was there a dull moment.

Yes, I enjoy observing/photographing virtually all manners of flora and fauna. Yes, I've been able to find beauty in any landscape of my travels. Yes, the pursuit of dramatic, memorable light is an exciting process. But the privilege and pleasure of being able to capture some of the magic that emanates from the white deer; spirit deer, has changed my life.

Lighthouses of the Great Lakes

BY Terry Pepper

Born in the England in 1948, Terry learned a deep respect for both history and photography before emigrating to North America with his family in 1964. Taking a lakeside drive from Indiana to the family lake cottage near Traverse City in 1994, the couple stopped to take some photos of lighthouses for some friends back in Indiana. Smitten by the serene beauty of these historical structures, the couple photographed sixteen lighthouses over the next six days, and were "hooked." After subsequent field trips, Terry created his non-commercial website "Seeing The Light" in 1998, which is dedicated to sharing the rich history of the lights of lakes Superior, Michigan and Huron. Terry serves as a Director of the Great Lakes Lighthouse Keepers Association, and is a member of a number of Great Lakes lighthouse preservation groups,. He gives presentations on lighthouse history throughout the Great Lakes area, and has assisted various lighthouse groups with historical and technical research of their lighthouses, and his photography has been featured in a number of publications.

HARBOR BEACH

Work began on the "Million Dollar Harbor" at what was then known as Sand Beach in 1873 in order to create a harbor of refuge for vessels sailing along the unprotected 115-mile stretch of coastline between Port Huron and Saginaw Bay. The Harbor Beach Light was established on the north end of the entry into the harbor in 1885 to guide mariners into the opening in the breakwaters, which are both detached from the shore. As such, the lighthouse is only accessible by boat, and we arranged to take a tour of the structure with a representative of the Harbor Beach Lighthouse Preservation Society, which has been actively engaged in restoring the structure for a number of years. The immensity of the harbor construction project becomes clear when viewed from the station's lantern, far out on the breakwater.

POINTE AUX BARQUES

With Pointe aux Barques marking an important turning point for vessels entering and leaving Saginaw Bay, the Federal government established the first light on the point in 1848. However, as a result of shoddy materials and workmanship, the structure deteriorated quickly, and was replaced by the existing tower and dwelling in 1857. Now a county park, we arrived at the station on a sunny day in early May before the park opened for the summer season and before the leaves on the many trees had filled-out to a point that they intruded on obtaining an open views of the station. With the entire grounds to ourselves, we were able to enjoy both the wide vista of Huron's turquoise waters and the many wildflowers that were pushing their way to the surface to stake their claim on the new season.

POTTAWATOMIE

The Pottawatomie Light station was established in 1839, and sits at northernmost end of Rock Island atop a 120-foot cliff with a commanding view of the passage into Green Bay between Rock and St, Martin Islands. Visiting the light was the culmination of a half-day odyssey which began at 7.00 AM at Gills Rock at the northerly end of the Door Peninsula, where we caught the first ferry of the day to take us across Deaths Door to Washington Island. A leisurely drive northward across Washington Island took us to the old

fishing village of Jackson Harbor where we abandoned our vehicle and boarded the small passenger ferry for the 20-minute trip to the southern tip Rock Island. After donning our backpacks, we made the enjoyable 1-mile hike along the bluffs around the western shore of the island to the lighthouse, which sits in a clearing amid apple trees and lilac bushes planted by the station's keepers 150 years ago – a wonderful spot for the picnic lunch we had carried all morning.

SOUTH HAVEN

The little red lighthouse at the pierhead in South Haven was erected in 1903 to replace a timber-framed beacon which had served to guide mariners between the piers at the entrance to the Black River since 1872. As is the case today with most of the harbors along Michigan's western shore, the piers serve as a gathering place, with locals using the piers as a convenient fishing location, and visitors walking their length to experience the inebriating combination of fresh breezes and sunshine. While this photograph shows the lake on a calm and sunny September morning, the elevated "catwalk" running along the center of the pier serves as a stark reminder of less peaceful days when dedicated keepers carefully clung to the hand rails as they made their way along the pier to tend the light, as 10-foot icy waves crashed over the surface of the pier.

ST JOSEPH

The first lighthouse, a wooden dwelling with a tower on the gable roof was established at St. Joseph to guide mariners into the river in 1859. After piers were erected to prevent the river from constant silting, the existing pair of structures were erected at the turn of the 20th century to form a range, whereby vessels could ascertain the channel into the river by lining them up so one light appeared directly above the other. While modern technology has largely eliminated the need for the lights to all but pleasure boaters that call St. Joseph home, hundreds of visitors throng to the beach and piers on summer evenings to enjoy the light shows which frequently erupt as the setting sun paints the entire western horizon in amazing pastel hues.

SAND ISLAND

The Apostle Islands are arrayed like jewels off Bayfield Peninsula on the southwestern shore of Lake Superior. As the "gateway to the Apostles," the village of Bayfield once served as a home base for a large fleet of fish tugs which worked the fertile passages between the islands, but today serves the many tourists who throng the village's restaurants and gift shops. After the opening of the Sault Canal in 1855, the flow of vessels making their way along Superior's south shore exploded, by 1891, six lighthouses were established on The Apostles to help guide mariners around the islands. The light-house at Sand Island was established in 1881, and is arguably one of the most beautiful of them all. Built of sandstone quarried on one of the islands, the little station sits on a rocky point at the north end of the island. Without a dock at the station, our only access to the station was to bring the bow of the boat up to the rocks and make a quick jump. This photo-graph was taken during one of two unsuccessful trips to the island, when wave action precluded our precluded our mak-ing the "leap of faith." Fortunately, the next day, the lake laid flat, and we were able to tour the building from top to bottom.

CRISP POINT

Established in 1904 to bridge a gap along Superior's "Shipwreck Coast," Crisp Point was a first-class light station with duplex brick dwelling, fog signal building, barns and storage buildings to support the graceful tower. No longer serving any purpose, the station support buildings were demolished by the Coast Guard In 1965, leaving the tower as silent witness to the dedicated keepers who called Crisp Point home. The lakeshore on which the tower stands is magnificent in its desolation, with the surf-swept beaches void of any signs of humanity for miles in each direction beyond the occasional agate-hunter. The desolation is furthered by the trip out to the light, which winds through 5 miles of single-track seasonal roads. Just hope you don't encounter any oncoming traffic, as places where two vehicles can pass are few and far between.

STURGEON BAY

One of Lake Michigan's famous red lighthouses, so painted to conform to the "red, right, returning" standard, the Ship Canal Pierhead light stands isolated from the main pier, and accessed by a cast ion catwalk. We arrived at the light station early one September morning with hopes of photographing the station silhouetted against the rising sun. Dismayed, our plans our early morning plans appeared for naught, as clouds shrouded the lake to the east, and old sol never made an appearance. As we were packing up our equipment to leave, the crewmembers of the Coast Guard Cutter Sundew arrived and headed out along the catwalk. We set up our equipment again, and captured the shot above showing the seamen working on the station.

SPLIT ROCK

Established in 1910, Split Rock Light station is located atop a 140-foot cliff which looms over the north shore of Lake Superior, and is arguably one of the most beautiful of all stations throughout the Great Lakes. We had looked forward to visiting this station for a number of years, since it is over 700 miles from our home. The drive along highway 61 was enjoyable, clinging as it does to the side of the lake, and passing through an unexpected tunnel and by a number of impressive waterfalls. We almost missed our first view of the station, which can be seen from a clearing in the trees about a mile to the east, forcing us to turn around and pull off the road to enjoy the view. In fact, we sat on the tailgate of our truck , and ate the picnic lunch as we gazed at the lighthouse perched atop the cliff. Arriving at the station, we immediately headed down the long wooden stairway to the lakeshore and took the photograph shown before making the arduous climb back up the stairs to explore the station buildings.